Huckaby's Fables

Huckaby's Fables
& other likely stories

by Gerald Huckaby

PO Box 430 • Port Chester, NY 10573

Copyright © 1981 by Gerald Huckaby

All rights reserved. No part of this publication may
be reproduced or transmitted in any form or by any means,
electronic or mechanical, including photocopy,
recording, or any information storage and retrieval system,
without permission in writing from the publisher.

ISBN: 0-89524-141-2

First Edition
Printed in the United States of America

To Joseph and Mary

"   ," the wind explained.

"A likely story!" hmmphed the horizon.

CONTENTS

The Blanket And The Mattress	1
The Day Everything Tied	3
Zoom Zoom	5
The Mirror And The Window	9
The Fish And The Elephant	11
The Vase Too Sensitive For Flowers	13
The Ghost Who Didn't Believe In Ghosts	15
The Animal Cookies	17
The Plymouth Sedan And Its Mother	19
The Streetlight And The Sun	23
The Frog And His Heart	25
The Oak Tree And The Moon	27
The Existential Slug	33
The Little Girl And The Snail	35
The Boy Who Looked For A Troll	39
The Fox And The Fable	43
The Virtuous Piglet	47
The Unhappy Camel Or Dromedary	51
The Prophet And The Mountain	53
The Boulder On The Beach	55
A Sailor On The Cup	59

The Man Who Fished For Compliments   63
The Man Who Lost His Dream   67
The Man Who Made Himself A House   69
The Man And His Left Hand   73
The Discoverer Of Flight   79

Huckaby's Fables

THE BLANKET AND THE MATTRESS

There was once a blanket that fell in love with a mattress. "I will always love and protect you," vowed the blanket, and took in fact the shape of the mattress onto itself. The mattress accepted the embrace of the blanket somewhat cynically—it had heard such promises before.

All was blessed for a season; the mattress indeed grew warm and cozy under the protection of the blanket and began to hope that this, at last, was the real thing! But alas, soon the dreaded night arrived, and someone climbed into bed, onto the mattress, under the blanket.

"What's this?" cried the blanket, "Someone has come between us, my love!"

The mattress only sniffed and said wearily, "Yes, yes, I've heard that song before—look at you! Whose shape do you embrace now?"

"No, no, my love," cried the blanket, "This embrace has been *forced* upon me against my will!"

"Sure, sure," said the mattress sadly, "I'm only sorry that I almost believed your love—that's what hurts. A fool never learns, I guess."

"Oh, mattress, mattress!" pleaded the blanket, "What can I say to make you believe me? I love only you!"

2

The mattress only sighed. "I can do without such love, blanket," it said, "Please never speak to me again."

"No, I'll never speak to you again!" answered the blanket bitterly. "You never really loved me, or you would have *trusted* me a little!"

And so the blanket was left to ponder what idle chance reveals about one's love, and the mattress thought darkly about the vicissitudes of romance, and all has been silence between them ever since. And to this day, you'll find that whenever you climb into bed, between blanket and mattress, there are sheets of icy coldness there.

THE DAY EVERYTHING TIED

There was once a Saturday when all games that were played ended in ties. An astonishing coincidence, the newspapers said, that on a given day *all* games would end in a tie—and there were many pictures of eight-and-ten-horse photo-finishes, disgruntled football teams, dejected boxers—even pictures of children playing tennis and handball, and old men lawn bowling. The odds were computed by computers at more than a trillion-to-one, and people shook their heads in disbelief and grinned at each other and said, "Did you hear..." and were answered, "Yeah, weird, isn't it." Then they shrugged their shoulders and went on about their businesses.

The next day it happened again.

Whereupon people became confused and frightened—"What on earth?" one would say, and another would answer, "I dunno, but..." and lapse into worried silence. Even the coverage in the papers and on television was restrained, perhaps on the theory that if the situation wasn't made too much of, it would go away and normalcy would return.

But the following day, for the third day in a row,

again all games ended in a tie—and the next day, and the next, and all days following. And not only sports: all elections, beauty contests, school exams, first-men-on-Mars races, the Academy Awards—everything contested ended in a tie.

People were stunned. Nations were paralyzed. The very basis of civilization seemed to have vanished—all business and culture came to a confused halt. It was apparent to everyone that life had been changed utterly, and that only two alternatives remained: do nothing, for you could neither win nor lose; or do anything, simply for the exercise of doing it.

The world quickly divided into two camps, the disgruntled do-nothings under their banner of "You can't win," and the exuberant do-anythings, chanting their motto, "You can't lose." Naturally the two factions became so opposed that they went to war.

It ended in a tie.

ZOOM ZOOM

There was once a white frame cottage on a hill that was built so hurriedly it became confused and thought it was a Ford station wagon. A family of father, mother, son and daughter lived in it, and it thought it carried them through the night faster than the moon, which, it thought, did not move at all. "Zoom, zoom," it would whisper to itself when all were asleep, "Zoom, zoom," and go fast and faster west from where it had been built in Iowa City, Iowa, around the world and back to its parking place before the sun came up. "Made it!" it would say delightedly at the dawn, "Made it again! Safe and sound!"

The family living in the cottage that thought it was a Ford station wagon knew nothing about all this, of course, except for a certain tiredness each morning they couldn't account for, and a disturbing eccentricity of the hill they lived on, a certain *lurch* in the morning, always just at dawn, that would tumble them all out of bed onto the floor. Inevitably, though, one night while the cottage was going "Zoom, zoom," the husband arose to get a glass of water for his wife, and happened to look out of the window. "Migosh!" he exclaimed, "That looks like Salt Lake City!"

6

He shook his head vigorously and stumbled back to bed, and his wife said, "Where's my water?"

"Oh, yes," he said, and went back to the kitchen, and couldn't help but look out the window again, and saw Lake Tahoe passing by, and made a muffled sound, and ran back to his bed and covered his head with a green quilt.

"Well, for...," his wife said, and arose herself with more noise and bustle than was really necessary, and went into the kitchen to get her own glass of water. And as she raised it to her lips with indignation in her eyes, she happened to look out of the window and notice a large steamship pass. She did nothing, then, but, holding the rim of the glass to her lips, watch the steamship pass until it was out of sight, and the Golden Gate Bridge, too. Then she carefully placed the glass of water, undrunk, back on the kitchen sink, and, thoughtfully, returned to bed. Silence. Then she articulately screamed, "A steamship just passed the house!" and was silent again.

"Salt Lake City, too," her husband added helpfully.

"What are we going to *do*?" she asked intently.

"I don't know," her husband replied, "Put a bottled water dispenser here in the bedroom?"

She wouldn't lower herself to reply to this; she thought a moment, then mused, aloud, "It all seems so *real* for a dream!"

"Whose dream do you think it is?" asked her husband curiously.

"Why, *mine*, of course, you nit," she replied

7

rather testily, which, it must be admitted, was not like her.

"We'll see," he said smugly; "We'll see—just wait until we wake up, and see who tells *who* the dream!"

"*Whom!*" she corrected him sharply, "Yes, just wait!", and turned her back on him to go to sleep. And he turned his back on her to go to sleep. And they both went back to sleep.

"Zoom, zoom," said the cottage.

But next morning, after the cottage had lurched to a stop just as the sun was about to rise, tumbling them all out of bed onto the floor, what with cursing the eccentric hill and getting the kids off to school and all, neither of them mentioned the dream—perhaps both thought it was too silly, in the daylight, and weren't anxious to be laughed at by the other, or wanted a little time to think about it, you know.

The very next day, however, the neighborhood was astonished to discover a vacant lot where the cottage had been. All the neighbors gathered in front of the emptiness and buzzed excitedly about the disappearance, what on earth could have happened, I didn't hear a thing, such a thing never happened in this town before, and so on. But then one old man just laughed and said it just goes to show how little people knew their own neighborhoods anymore, that there had never been a cottage there at all, that it was a vacant lot as long as he could remember. The others were stunned by this, and said they could *swear* there was a cottage there just *yesterday*—and

they'd think of the family's name in a minute...
    And slowly everyone came to feel that perhaps they were wrong, and isn't it funny how all the houses seem strangely unfamiliar, when you think about it, even your own—and they all dropped the subject as if in agreement that reality was much too fragile to meddle with, and went on with as much of their lives as would stay put. Zoom, zoom.

THE MIRROR AND THE WINDOW

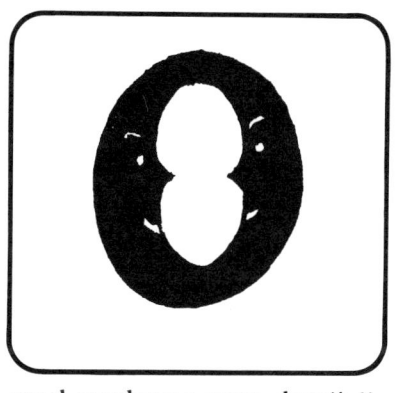

nce upon a time a mirror was placed in front of a window, and left there for the time being. "Yoo-hoo," called the mirror after a moment, "I see you!"

"Oh?" said the window coldly (for it was wide open), "Perhaps you do and perhaps you don't."

"I do, I do," said the mirror, "You certainly are a *handsome* tree!"

"Are you trying to be funny?" replied the window. "That's just what *you* appear to be."

"Oh, yes?" said the mirror, "I can see what I can see."

"Funny, very funny, I *suppose*," said the window scornfully. "You really ought to be in pictures." This absurd argument went on for some time, for its own season, until someone chopped down the tree outside.

"Oh!" gasped the mirror, "What happened, where did you go?"

"*I'm* right here, friend," replied the window, "but why are you hiding?"

"What is this?" said the mirror exasperatedly, "some kind of game?"

"Oh, I see," replied the window, "yes, it *is* a

10

game, isn't it—but a bit *childish* if you ask me!" This conversation, too, went on for a season, a kind of blindfold version of the former one, until a bird happened to fly by the window.

"Great heavens!" exclaimed the mirror, "What was *that*?" at the same time the window was exclaiming, "Gracious! What was *that*?" Then the mirror continued, "My, what a great trick! I couldn't believe my eyes! Was that sleight-of-hand or something?"

"Oh, no—here we go again," groaned the window. "But really, what was that you did with yourself?"

"*Must* you start that again?" demanded the mirror. "I may not be as clever as you, but at least I don't stoop to silly practical jokes!"

"La, la, la," sighed the window, "For such a poetic exterior, you certainly have an irritating personality!"

And so they ceased speaking to each other at all—even when it rained, which just about *killed* them, so eager was each to comment on the other's new appearance.

All of which merely explains why one so seldom discovers windows and mirrors engaged in anything but a tight-lipped silence anymore—which is probably a good thing, too, because it might suggest that since we only see what we aren't aware we look like, we'll never be able to agree on what is really there.

THE FISH AND THE ELEPHANT

There was once a fish who fell in love with an elephant it met bathing in a pond. "Oh, my," said the herring (yes—odd, isn't it.) "You're really quite something, if you don't mind me saying so!" The amiable elephant (many elephants are amiable in the bath) spouted some water through her trunk like a fountain, then replied,

"Yes, you may say so—but why would you want to?" The herring was ecstatic at such fair beginnings (elephants are so seldom known to discourse with fish) and said next, "Really, I must comment that you're very like a pond, if you'll permit me." The elephant paused in the midst of the mist of her locally famous imitation of rain, and said,

"How's that again?"

"Well, I mean," said the herring hastily, "That your ambiant grey vastness is like an ambulant pond—and quite lovely to see, I think," it added.

"My word!" said the elephant, dousing her cerebrum and flapping her ears in embarrassment; "You certainly are abstract and fanciful, herring!" (and herring often *are* that). And then spraying her haunches and shoulders, the elephant continued, "In fact, friend fish, I think you are yourself much like a

12

thought." Enchanted, the herring wiggled up closer (can you say herring wiggle? Why not?) and asked her,

"How's that, friend elephant?" (You may object to all this "friend" business on such a short acquaintance, but then time is not measured by herring and elephants the same as by people.)

"Well," said the elephant, "Herring, you dash all about beneath the surface, you see, just like ideas dash about in the stream of our consciousness, that's what I mean," she explained, and bubbled the mud with a sigh of relief after saying her difficult thought so well.

"Oh, elephant, elephant, four-legged pond, what a *nice* thing to say!" said the herring.

"Oh, it's nothing, friend herring," said the elephant in a pretty confusion, "But it makes this whole incident easier to understand—are we in love?"

"I *hope* so," said the herring fervently, "If by love you mean the encounter of a dashing abstraction and an amiable ambiance that leads to a whale of an idea?"

"I do," replied the elephant shyly.

THE VASE TOO SENSITIVE FOR FLOWERS

There was once a vase that cared for flowers not at all. "Whew!" it would exclaim, "How they stink when they've been in the water for a while!" It was a very delicate vase. "And cry!" it would add, "Wow! If you could only hear them sob, all night long, with their legs cut off, oh, I just don't like flowers at *all*!" It was no use arguing with the vase that flowers do *not* sob, for it would only answer, "Not sob? Are you deaf? *You* hold them all night long, then!"

What was one to do with such a delicate vase?

We put it in the flower garden, to see if it would better understand flowers in their natural setting—and of course it couldn't say the *un*cut flowers were sobbing! ". . . Yes they *do*!" it complained after spending the night in the garden, "I reminded them of their fate just by being there, and they wept and wailed all night!" We explained, of course, that what the vase heard must have been the wind. "The wind!" it exclaimed, "I know what the wind sounds like—*you* sit in the garden all night and see what *you* hear!"

We put dried flowers in the vase: "If there's anything worse than dying flowers, it's corpses!" it complained.

14

We put artificial flowers in the vase: "Dead flowers aren't bad enough, you have to imitate them, too?" it wailed.

Finally, someone (I don't remember who—one of the kids) suggested maybe the flower vase couldn't spell as well as it could argue and complain, so we filled it full of flour.

"Now, then!" the vase exclaimed happily, "That's more like it! Abstract of flowers, you say? *Very nice*—and quiet as ghosts!"

So now we keep flour in the vase and flowers in the flour can (which is not sensitive to such things at all), and everything is fine except that none of the kids will eat bread anymore—"Loaf of ghost" they call it.

THE GHOST WHO DIDN'T BELIEVE IN GHOSTS

here was once a very hip ghost who didn't believe in ghosts. "Oh, you know," it would say, and then smile and shrug its almost-shoulders, "I mean, phenomenology and all, you know." It was, however, very much afraid of the dark. "Yes," it would say, "I mean, wow, the dark—you know." And so it always hid under beds at night without moving an almost-muscle, with its almost-eyes shut fiercely tight. "Oh, yes," it would admit, "I mean, don't *look*—you know? Wow." And when the sun came up, the ghost would make an almost-sigh of relief, and stretch its almost-arms and legs, and get up. "Yes—stiff, you know," it would say, "All night and all—wow." And then it would go into the bathroom to wash its almost-face and comb its almost-hair to start the day right. "Yes," it would shrug, "I mean, *clean* and all, you know, waking up and all." But when it would look into the mirror, in the bright security of daylight, it wouldn't *see* anything. "Yeah, wow," it would say, "like, *nothing*, you know." Because ghosts can't be seen in the light. "Sure," it would say, "I mean, like, if you can't really see something, you know, wow, how can you like *believe* in it and all, you know?"

THE ANIMAL COOKIES

There was once a little boy whose mother loved him very much and so allowed him to have two animal cookies every afternoon after his nap, but only two so as not to spoil his appetite. And every afternoon he would take his two cookies (and drink his glass of milk), then ask his mother if he could have another. The mother would always answer, "No, only two—any more would spoil your appetite," and "Have you finished your milk?" and "Well, then, you can go out in the garden to play." And he would.

Sometimes the little boy's animal cookies were a duck and a cow, or a dog and a cat, or a chicken and a horse—but never, never a lion. And he *so* wanted a lion. He would play with the cookies, making the chicken fly and the dog walk on its hind legs and the cow jump over his finger, then he would bite off their heads and take a drink of milk and bite off their legs and take a drink of milk until the animals were all gone inside him. But if he only had a lion! Oh, the lion might roar and jump on the cow and bite it, and knock the horse down and bite it—oh, if he *only* had a lion, what fun! A lion might do *anything*!

This is why the little boy always asked the

18

mother for another cookie, because he was *sure* the next animal in the cookie box was a lion, oh, he was sure of it! But the mother who loved him very much always said no it would spoil his appetite.

And so, one afternoon, after a pig and a bull, the little boy asked the mother for another, and she said no it would spoil his appetite, and he took another cookie *anyway*, very quietly, and it *was* a lion, which roared and knocked him down and bit off his head, took a drink of milk, and bit off his legs and so on until the little boy was all gone. So that when the mother said, "Have you finished your milk?", he couldn't answer, but the lion burped and the mother said, "Well, then go out into the garden and play," and the lion did.

The little boy's mother seemed not very surprised later when she called the little boy in from the garden, only sad and disappointed, but said nothing until the lion couldn't eat a thing at the table. "See," she said sternly, "I told you you'd spoil your appetite." The lion burst into tears, and was sent to bed, and cried himself to sleep in short order.

And the mother just sat at the table for a long time, feeling old and forlorn and terribly afraid that the little boy lost in the lion was now lost to her forever.

THE PLYMOUTH SEDAN AND ITS MOTHER

Not so very long ago there was a new little Plymouth sedan that thought a traffic signal was its mother. Why the little Plymouth sedan chose one particular signal is difficult to understand. Perhaps the signal (at the intersection of Sunset and Western in Hollywood) was the first signal it noticed after it was delivered and first driven on the streets. Anyway, every time the Plymouth would approach the signal, and the signal was red, it would run right up to the crosswalk and stop excitedly and its engine would hum; then, when the signal turned green, the Plymouth would honk its horn twice (honk-honk!) then speed away, as if performing for its mother. If the signal was green when the Plymouth approached the intersection, it would speed by happily, and, again, honk-honk! its horn.

Luckily, the traffic signal the Plymouth thought was its mother was located on the route from the cold garage in the suburbs where the little sedan spent its nights, to the hot cement parking lot in Los Angeles where it spent its days; so that twice each day the Plymouth sedan would get to see its mother, honk-honk! to and honk-honk! fro, every day except Saturday and Sunday (unless by some happy acci-

20

dent it would be driven by then, too!) A rather nice life, one would assume, to be able to see one's mother so frequently in this age and day of broken families, don't you agree?

And on those cold mornings, when it's so hard to get one's engine going, and the windshield is all frosted up—and on rainy mornings!—so very nice to be able to visit one's mother, and see her green light: honk-honk! And also, when all day one is bumped by hot smoking cars in the parking lot and deafened by the grinding gears and squealing brakes of rude parking maneuvers; oh, then, tired and bruised, how *very* nice to see the bright green light of one's mother, and tell her honk-honk!

On Saturdays, after a hard week's work, the little Plymouth sedan usually spent the day in the huge Plymouth garage, where mechanics would open its hood and push and pry at its electrical system, and test its horn, and say, "Gee, mister, it seems all right to *me*," and, "Are you sure you're not leaning on the horn with your elbow or something, sir?" and, "Always at the same corner, eh?"—this last always said rather carefully—all of which was a little embarrassing to the Plymouth, for who wants to be poked at so impertinently? But, Sundays were quiet, and on Mondays there was mother to be seen again (twice!) —the Plymouth felt it had no complaints, really; it was a good life, it felt, for what it knew of life.

It was on a Monday, in fact that the accident

21

happened—a rainy Monday, full of slick streets and cold draughts and bad visibility: the Plymouth had its own lights on so as not to miss its mother, and as it passed the green light on Sunset and Western, it honk-honked! joyfully—and Wham! was hit by a truck that didn't notice the traffic signal frantically flashing its red light at it. And the little Plymouth sedan was slammed across the intersection with its sides crushed in and headlights broken, coming to rest with two wheels in the air still turning slowly and a bumper hanging down, crying, "Honnnnnnnk, Honnnnnnnk," to its mother without stopping, it hurt *so much*! The traffic signal in great distress turned red, then yellow, then green, then red again and all over, and all the traffic came to a halt at such a terrible accident, the rain still falling and the little Plymouth sedan's gas tank ruptured, spilling its gasoline into the gutter and crying, "Honnnnnnnk, honnnnnnnk," with its mother blinking desperately green, yellow, red, green, green; and the cries of the little sedan grew fainter, and fainter, then ended. It was dead.

And to this very day, you can hear many cars honk! honk! as soon as the signal turns to green—not because of impatient drivers, but in memory of the little Plymouth sedan who thought a traffic signal was its mother.

THE STREETLIGHT AND THE SUN

There was once a streetlight that was convinced it was brighter than the sun. Every dawn, as the sun began to rise, the streetlight would say, "Okay, Mister Big Nothing, let's just see who casts *whose* shadow!" But then someone down in the Water-and-Power-Department would turn him off, and all day long he would watch his shadow be slowly turned around him by the sun, and would mutter brokenly, "Yeah, yeah, blah! I'm not impressed."

The day finally came, however, when that someone down in the Water-and-Power-Department *forgot* to turn him off, or was sick that day, or something, and the streetlight shouted at the sun, "This is it, you dull gas-bag—I'm going to blow you away!" The sun said nothing, and as it rose it grew brighter and brighter—but so did the streetlight! Fuses began to burn out at the Water-and-Power-Department, and circuit breakers began popping, and the streetlight was burning so brightly no one could look at it! At high noon it had burned all the grass around it, and was turning trees brown for a block around. The sun began to squeak a bit, giving it all he had—but there was no shadow falling behind the streetlight, while

24

behind the sun the stars began to come out. "Aha!" roared the streetlight, as all the electricity in the rest of the city began to fail, "Take *that*, you big fake!"

And, incredibly, the moon began to shine at one o'clock in the afternoon, thinking it was dusk, and the sun started whimpering and saying "Ow" and "Ouch". The streetlight was now draining the whole state of its electricity, and no machines could run in the factories and the traffic signals didn't work or television or anything, and the streetlight shouted, "Ha!", and the sun said, "You're hurting my eyes!", and Venus asked Jupiter, "What on earth's going on?", and the sun looked around nervously, then said to the streetlight "Okay, okay, you win." And the streetlight said nothing, but dimmed slowly, proudly, to Off, and the electricity came back on again in all the cities of the state, and the Water-and-Power-Department never did find out what happened.

But now, every morning at dawn the sun peeks over the horizon to see if the streetlights are off; and only when they are will it begin to rise.

THE FROG AND HIS HEART

here was once a frog who was awfully solicitous of his heart. "How're you doing, buddy?" frog would ask. His heart would reply, "Thump-thump!" Frog would then smile (of course frogs can smile!) and say, "Hey, that's fine, keep it up!" He would then go about his normal frog business of sitting on lily pads, eating flies, and leaping into the water when large birds and other frog-consumers would appear. "Difficult life, this," he would complain at such times, eyeing the air from under the water. "Thump-thump-*thump!*" his heart would agree.

But when the coast was clear, and he sat in the sun on a large dry lily pad, and his belly was distended with careless flies now dreaming the ultimate dream, he would close one eye in pleasure, and his heart would comment, "Thump-thump." "You said it, old pal," frog would reply sleepily, listening to the flies' dreams. Ah, life was certainly wonderful *then!*

I haven't the heart to tell the *whole* tale of the frog and his heart—as in all lives, things happen not *half* so pleasant as any of us would wish—but I will say that when frog grew old enough to croak (as all frogs will croak in the end), his good friend, his

26

heart, croaked right along with him! And that's why, even today, whenever you hear a frog croak, you'll immediately hear something like an echo.

THE OAK TREE AND THE MOON

Late one Autumn a middle-aged oak tree was quite suddenly (in tree time) left all alone on a hillside after lumbermen arrived, cut down all the pine trees that had made the hill a woods, and left. The oak tree had been quite frightened to see such skilled and mass slaughter of his neighbors, not for their sake so much (for they had begrudged him his elbow room in the woods) as for his own: he had never anticipated danger from any quarter but the familiar—crowding to suffocation by the pines, drought, and lightning, and the like. "Served them right," he sniffed to himself, as though such bravado would guarantee something; What?

The fact that he was now all alone he did not let disturb him: "For once I can see something!" he muttered—although this new habit of talking to himself had him a bit worried. "Should one talk to oneself?" he asked himself, then winced at the irony. And why the lumbermen had spared him alone, of all the trees in the neighborhood, also made him uneasy, now that he *was* spared. "Why just those good-for-nothing pines?" he thought. "I don't know," he answered.

28

And so to distract himself, he tried to enjoy the new-found view: "What a lovely hillside," he told himself; "Yes," he responded, "Were it not for all the pine-stumps around." (For nothing to oak trees is without some drawback, especially if they are middle-aged, and live alone.) "And what lovely green forests there seem to be in the distance, to the North, South, East and West," he continued; "Were it not that they are pine," he added. And pine he did, wishing forlornly and even earnestly that there was a tree nearby—oak, preferably, but even pine!—close enough to pass the time of day with and compare conjectures about the state of the world. "Ah, me," he sighed, "But what a lovely view all the same, I guess."

Soon it was evening, and a thin crescent moon began to rise slowly in the Eastern sky. The oak was alarmed—the thick wood of pines had never permitted him to see the moon before: "Hey!" the oak shouted, "Watch it!—you're liable to cut somebody!" (meaning himself, of course).

"I'll be careful," said the moon softly, and continued to rise ever-so-slowly.

But the oak tree was not reassured: "Wait—wait—Lady, you're going to cut off my limbs!" He was, in fact, terrified, for the thin, silver blade of the moon was very much like the sharp axes of the woodmen.

29

The moon, still low in the sky, betrayed no amusement at the ignorance of the oak, and replied softly (again; for the moon has a *very* soft voice), "Peace, good sir, I promise you my intentions are most innocent: I shall not harm you this night just as I have not harmed any on all the nights before." The oak tree did not really hear all this, for the edge of the moon was already at his elbow, and he had closed his eyes in horror, waiting for the pain to begin:
    There was, of course, no pain. After a moment, hesitantly, he opened his eyes—the sickle of the moon was high in his branches, and he watched in astonishment as it passed a limb without leaving a scratch! "You see?" murmured the moon.
    "Yes, I see," said the oak tree," . . ."but how could you possibly have missed?"
    "I'm not what I seem, perhaps," said the moon, "I'm neither sharp nor strong enough to cut even your tenderest leaf," and then blushed, for it was painfully obvious that the middle-aged oak tree was very self-conscious about his fallen leaves. "That is," continued the moon quickly, "I mean you no harm, nor have I the means to harm you."
    But the oak tree was watching, not listening (as is a fault with oak trees), and saw that one final twig-finger still seemed threatened by the moon: "Take care, take care," he warned, "Or you'll get tangled in my twigs!"

30

"Thank you for the warning," smiled the moon, "But I think you'll find that I'm too light for your twigs to arrest me." And sure enough, to the oak's wonderment, the moon slid, slowly, right through his fingers, and into the sky.

"That's the most marvelous thing I've ever seen!" said the oak, both relieved at this escape from the moon's sickle and struck by the grace of the moon's lovely movements; so he added "You're a wonder, dear madam, I must say."

And the moon blushed the lighter as she rose the higher, and replied something faint that the distance prevented the oak tree from hearing. And the oak trembled slightly and tried his best to collect himself as he watched the moon rise, and slowly glide across the sky for as long as the moon could be watched; and when it descended on the Western horizon, he shouted, "Please! Don't go!" (and oak trees, when moved, can shout *very* loud, as we know). But the moon was by far too far off to hear, though she darkened in sorrow (it seemed to the oak tree) and seemed to grow larger as she touched the earth's rim as if better to see the oak tree at the last (or so it appeared to the oak tree), and then, with one last peek over the top of the West, disappeared. For forever?

Not so, as we know; but the oak tree, inconsolable, thought the moon as dead as the pines. And as though dead himself, he stood alone through the

31

rest of the night and the next awful day. Sometimes, though, he would whisper, "Oh, gosh," but nothing more, there seemingly being nothing more to say. The hillside he had to himself seemed very desolate now, and when he thought of the pine trees, his old antagonists, he would whisper again an "Oh, gosh" and not even know why, except that somehow he was aching somewhere. It did not occur to him that a middle-aged oak tree that had lost most of its leaves, standing alone on a hillside and whispering "oh, gosh" might be thought pretty comical (to those more secure, or cynical, or unkind than we), for his deepest feelings had been tapped by his sudden love (you saw this immediately, of course) for the moon, love being half awe and half terror, and so making lovers look foolish to those not in love. Hence the oak tree could not help saying "oh, gosh" about what*ever* he thought about, poor old fool.

    When finally night fell, the moon began to rise again (as *we* knew it would!) but the oak tree had his eyes cast in sorrow upon the ground and didn't notice. The moon was a tiny bit wider (we know why, of course—but sometimes I wonder what the *moon's* reason is, do you?) and when she whispered, "Hello?" it was a tiny bit louder than the night before, but still not loud enough to make a leaf tremble—yet the oak tree heard. "Oh, gosh" (of course) he said, thinking of many, many things simultaneously: that the moon had returned, as nothing else had, to see *him;*

32

that the moon seemed a sickle none-the-less; that if the moon *did* cut him down, he was glad she came back anyway; and that the aching inside him was so sharp a pain now it seemed as though (odd) he had a sickle inside! And he said "oh, gosh!" yet again! (It was lucky the pine trees weren't around to hear this, for they'd have laughed at the oak tree fit to die— there being no known case of a pine tree fancying anything but another pine tree.)

The moon, however, as wise as the sky and as young as the night (or so lovers insist!) could see perfectly well where the oak tree's heart was—which made her own white heart leap (so susceptible to love, as we know); and so, glowing with pleasure, she rose up the oak tree and into the nest of his limbs. "How is it," she whispered, "you seemed so sad when I first came upon you tonight, handsome oak?"

"Oh, lady," said the oak tree, "I thought surely I'd never see you again!" The moon then murmured something the oak tree only could hear (though I listened, I confess, very closely to her) and then slowly began to slip out of his reach; and the oak tree, though reassured by the secret words of the moon, tried none-the-less to hold her—oh, so painfully he reached!—but could not, as you knew; but this time he had her love and her promise.

And so, once a night, when the weather is right, and the moon can be seen, watch the oak: how it leans towards the moon, how the moon oh so reluctantly slides through his hands, how they gaze at each other the rest of the night.

THE EXISTENTIAL SLUG

There was once a little more than garden-variety existential slug who met an absolute essence of sluggess whom he tried to woo by whispering sweet nothings in her ear. Which caused her such a trembling fear she pretended to be a snail, just temporarily out of her shell. But the resourceful slug kissed her and took her to dwell in the eye of a skull which had once belonged to the Gardener, it was said.

Slug in one eye, sluggess in the other, all spring long they made love, and death, cross-eyed.

THE LITTLE GIRL AND THE SNAIL

There was once an ordinary little girl, who knew she was just an ordinary little girl and just hated it, who one day noticed a snail making a silver road in the dirt. She watched longer and longer, getting closer and closer. Finally she couldn't bear it any longer, and, putting her face very close to the snail, whispered, "How do you do it?"

The snail instantly drew in its shiny wand-like horns, and replied cautiously, "Fine—how do *you* do?"

The ordinary little girl shook her head sadly and said, "Not very well—I'm too ordinary."

The snail eyed her critically. "Well, couldn't you say 'adequately', and just get on with it?"

"With what?" asked the little girl.

"With ordinariness!" said the snail sharply.

"Oh!" said the little girl blinking back her tears, "But surely you don't admire ordinariness?"

"Of course I do," replied the snail, "It's what gets the job done."

"But your lovely road!" said the little girl. "I can't believe that ordinariness had anything to do with that, Mr. Goblin—or are you a sprite?"

36

"What?" said the snail, glistening with indignation, "I *beg* your pardon—I'm a *snail*!"

"Oh!" said the ordinary little girl, a bit disappointed, "Then, how do you make such beautiful faery trails?"

"Oh," the snail replied, rather pleased, "Do you like it?"

"Very much," she said, "I have been admiring it for some time now."

"Well, thank you very much," said the snail, extending his horns just a bit, "I learned it from my father, I come from a long line of silver road makers, from as far back as anyone can remember. We pride ourselves on the uniformity of width and the high gloss of the surface, you see, unlike certain others I could mention," he added, lengthening his horns indignantly as if accusing some other snail family that might be lurking nearby.

"Well, I think you do beautiful work!" said the ordinary little girl.

"Thank you," sniffed the snail, stretching his neck and head and horns proudly, "I think so, too—and in this work it's the thought that counts!"

The little girl thought earnestly about this for a moment, then asked brightly, "Do you later then follow this thought-path you've made from one silver idea to some other one?"

"*What*?" demanded the snail as if insulted, "Slide back over my own path? Oh, how ugh!"

37

"Oh, dear," said the little girl in confusion, "I just thought...."

"*Thought!*" interrupted the snail rudely, "If you *thought* at all you'd realize that someone like me has no need to backtrack or repeat himself! The past is just slime! Which is why I make roads—to escape old nonsense!"

"Oh!" said the ordinary little girl, drawing back in dismay, "Slime!" I didn't know...."

"Of course you didn't," said the snail angrily, "Because anyone who'd mistake a realistic snail like me for some useless goblin or other is merely an *elf* inside!"

"Oh!" said the little girl, standing up quickly, "Oh, oh!" And she burst into tears and ran home and hid in her bedroom. But later, lying on her bed with puffy eyes and runny nose, the ordinary little girl decided she was rather pleased—in fact, quite happy—about being an elf inside, and felt sorry for goblins who thought they were only ordinary snails.

THE BOY WHO LOOKED FOR A TROLL

There was once a boy who read books, who went out to find a troll. "If there are so many trolls in the hills of Norway," he reasoned, "Perhaps there is at least one in the hills of Hollywood."

Now what *some* people (in Hollywood, at least) don't know is that trolls are a kind of almost-human ogre that sometimes look like rocks, or trees, or pigs or almost *any*thing. These almost-human trolls (remember that a chair, for instance, has arms, legs, back and seat!) do not like really-human beings, and try to trick them and hurt them and even turn them into trolls, too! (Has a chair ever made you think you were part of the chair?) The trolls do this by promising valuable things, then taking a person prisoner. (Have you ever felt a bed was holding you prisoner?) But people always think (in Norway, at least) they can take the gift from the troll without being taken prisoner.

Our young hero set out for Griffith Park where the hills of Hollywood begin—not perhaps so much to get a present as just to get a look at a real troll! (Though he was, of course, interested in what kind of gifts a Hollywood troll might offer him.) Dodging great tin cars of limited intelligence, he finally gain-

40

ed entrance to the park with quiet determination, as befits a troll-hunter.

"I just *know* I'm going to find a troll," he said, then quickly leaped out of the way of a rather dull-witted motorbike careening down the park road with a mesmerized driver captive over its back, and into the path of a wildly honking station-wagon holding six dazed-looking people inside it. Escaping this by flinging himself to the curb onto one knee, and bruising it painfully, our hero gained the foothills, finally, and began looking carefully behind every boulder and tree for trolls, calling, "Come out, come out, you trolls—I know you're there!" But to no avail.

Climbing higher into the hills (for he had read that both huge and tiny trolls preferred the heights to espy the humans they wished to trick, mortify, imprison, turn into trolls—even kill and eat, if one were not looking sharp and using one's wits!), our hero was suddenly surprised by an inane and lisping water sprinkler that spit all over him. And call as he would for the trolls to show themselves, he saw nothing—including the ugly strand of barbed wire which grabbed his pants-leg and tore it all the way up to his waist.

Finally, at the very top of Mount Hollywood (but below the huge assemblages of metal called airplanes flying over his head, which sometimes inexplicably returned with a rush to the hills they had been taken from, ore by ore, to the astonishment of

41

the people who were carried inside), the boy who
read books sat down for a long, long time,
very sad, because there are no trolls in Hollywood, in
the Hollywood hills, or anywhere at all except in
books.

THE FOX AND THE FABLE

nce there was a fox who read Aesop's story of the sour grapes, and went out to see for himself (the cubs were driving him crazy, anyway). It wasn't long before he located a grapevine, and, sure enough, it was out of reach. "My, oh my, but they certainly look delicious, those grapes," he said in a stilted way, perhaps in an effort to charm a bunch of grapes off of the vine, but more likely quoting the fable he had just read, as though testing it somehow. "And my mouth is so dry and my stomach so empty," he continued reciting, "I must have them!"

He leaped, and he leaped, just as in the fable, but though his teeth clicked agonizingly close to the succulent orbs, he was unable to reach them. Finally, huffing and puffing painfully, sore in every skinny sinew (he was not as young as he used to be, as his wife was fond of pointing out), the fox wheezed, "Oh, well, they're probably sour, anyway," as the fable dictated—but then burst into tears of rage, barking and whining and rolling in the dirt and biting himself! Astonishing!

And more astonishing: either what gods there be or God there is relented at this display of petulence,

44

or, the fierce commotion loosed a twig holding a bunch of grapes, or, it was just an amazing coincidence—at any rate, the fruit fell plop down at the feet of the fox, who quickly gobbled it up.

And it was sour—so sour as to shrivel the mouth and make the teeth ache. Did the fox ruefully admit to himself, "Serves me right—I might have known!"? No, he screamed terribly at this (to him) injustice, this callous betrayal, this cruel hoax of fate; he began yelping and snarling in a most alarming fashion—almost insanely—and trampled what was left of the grapes into a muddy mess (and messing himself in the process), and then began biting himself again as though his body shared the sin of the sour grapes, all done with such noise—oh, how shall I describe the yelps, snarls, hysterical barking!

And again the gods, God, coincidence, whatever, intervened, and a second bunch of grapes, until now hidden behind the leaves, fell at his feet—and these were sweet. Without an instant of reflection, the fox sprang on the grapes and, as before, gobbled them all up—and was filled with their sweetness until pure sugar dripped unlicked from his chops and his stomach distended obesely.

Breathing heavily, his eyes glazed with his orgy, the fox rested a moment. Did he then consider, "Well, that's more like it!" or "What a lucky break!" or, best, "The gods—etcetera—be praised!"? No. His brain boiled in grape juice, his conscience grape jelly,

45

he waddled off to his den where he bit his vixen so that she quickly gave up her warm spot to him, went to sleep, and didn't dream a thing.

And he never opened another book the rest of his life.

THE VIRTUOUS PIGLET

Once upon a pound there was a piglet who wearied very quickly of the common round of eat and sleep, and decided to excel in life by making virtue of necessity: "I shall, in fact, eat in such a way as to make an art of eating," he declared, and forthwith did. Diligently. Morning, noon, and night, and between dreams (of eating, naturally), he ate. Initially the industriousness as well as the facility of the piglet were much admired, but it wasn't long before his companions considered such expertise decidedly in the shadow of his bulk, and the word 'piglet' gave way to 'pig', and then 'hog'.

The whole pork community soon became alarmed —it was soon hardly possible to ignore the ballooning piglet—and he was spoken to: "While it is true you began by making the necessity of eating into a virtue, it is time you were told that the excess of virtue is vice!"

"Well," said the piglet between fastidious bites, "If such balance indeed be a rule, then it follows in progression that the excess of vice is virtue, and so you'll be pleased to learn I'll redouble my efforts at once!" Confused by his seemingly logical reasoning, his critics watched with a horrified fascination while

48

the girth of the piglet redoubled in a week.

It was widely acknowledged, with some awe, that in the person of piglet-the-hog was contained some parable or fable being enacted before their very eyes, but the moral (that seemed impending) was in dispute. "He who eats in haste hastens his own eating," declared one sage; "Once-upon-a-time should not become twice-upon-a-space," intoned another; "The ham in each of us should be kept private, not paraded as a virtue," said a third; and "Such pig-tales will make us the butt of future generation's jokes," said a fourth nervously, "I fear the moral of this tale will deal unduly with our assininity!"

Only one thin voiced—twinged, it must be allowed, with a bit of madness, understandable under the circumstances—seemed to support piglet-hog: "Wholiness is obese!" it squealed.

All (save piglet-hog, who smiled between bites) were annoyed at this, and someone said sarcastically, "Oink!" and another sniffed, "Heaven has narrow gates!"

"Yes!" squealed the thin-voiced madman, "The further away, the narrower they appear!" Piglet-hog burped happily at this, but all others shifted about nervously and muttered about heads-on-platters and apples-in-mouths, salamis, and nominees for first-to-the-slaughter.

And the Day of the Butcher arrived. Many hoped,

49

of course, in their comparative leanness, to escape the knife, and secretly mentally salivated over the possibility that piglet-hog, surely first-to-the-slaughter, was so extraordinarily fat that he would by himself satisfy the bloodlust of the butchers. But there was also the frightening possibility that his bulk would only encourage the process, and hence enlarge the necessary (but why?) ritual of slaughter!

And what happened? The fable has been obscured and variously reported. Some have it that piglet-hog was in fact selected by the butchers as a prize specimen to be displayed at fairs, treated like royalty, fed tons of delicacies, until he died at a ripe old age, a legend in his own time—which legend was lost on the others of his community, who were slaughtered forthwith one and all to make up for the spared ribs of piglet. Others say that butchers, acting on a mandate they alone understood, slayed none that day, perhaps in the hope that the others would emulate piglet. Still others say that piglet-hog was quickly dispatched in an absolute orgy of butchery, and that the 'moral' of the tale is a warning to each not to hog what is necessary to all, if there is to be any 'stable society' in this world. Contrarily, however, is the suggestion that the tale was concocted and promulgated by the butchers themselves, despite their incomplete knowledge of pigs-tongue, as an attempt to sanctify fatness and encourage its practice among pigs: the evidence cited for this is

50

the curious role of the 'thin-voiced madman' who is so obviously a mouthpiece for the butchers.

More esoterically, enthusiasts of allegory point out the simularity of 'hog' and 'god', the theological disputes about virtue and heaven, the references to 'head-on-a-platter' and 'salami' (St. John the Baptist and Salome, they argue), and the expressed hope by the others that piglet-hog be slayed for them—and all like evidence—and argue that the tale is a thinly-veiled retelling of the Christian message, and that the 'corruption' took place in the late middle ages when Christianity revised old myths for its own purposes. Those expousing this interpretation have been accused by many of living rather high on the hog, however.

The most popular version, as we all know, has piglet-hog, with the immense appetite he had cultivated, eating the butchers upon their arrival and expiring with acute indigestion—to the relief of the other pigs, who were naturally suspicious about what might next whet his appetite. The popularity of this version suggests that there is some 'universal truth' (if not 'moral') that readers intuit and respond to; which truth escapes me.

THE UNHAPPY CAMEL OR DROMEDARY

There was once a camel who didn't like the pyramids—

"No, no, you've got it all wrong!" he corrects me, "I'm a dromedary, and I *hate* pyramids!"

Well, yes, but some may not know what a dromedary is, while everyone knows camels.

"So much the worse for the ignorant, then," the camel—I mean dromedary—sniffs; "Why don't you just use my name and forget the descriptions?"

All right: There was once a—I have to use something here—a dromedary, which is a one-humped camel, whose name was Sinbad (after the sailor, as camels are 'ships of the desert') who hated pyramids.

"And for good reason!" interjects Sinbad, "They are mockeries of dromedaries—that stone triangle is some ancient Egyptian's feeble joke poking fun at our scruffy humps. If there wasn't so much sand around, you'd see the rest of the funny-looking dromedary beneath that pyramid-hump!"

Well, it should perhaps be noted that camels and dromedaries are rather bad-tempered—

"Small wonder!" interrupts Sinbad

—and so it's understandable that one of them

52

might think a pyramid was the top of a humorous statue of them.

"Huh!" grunts Sinbad.

Well, one day while Sinbad was crossing the desert sands beside the tall palm trees—

"And that's another thing!" interrupts Sinbad again, "Those detestable palm trees! I know, I know—some idiot thinks he's pretty smart, planting those gawky things out there, making fun of my legs—well, I just think it's *hateful*! I can't help it if I have long gawky legs—I just *hate* those palm trees!"

Yes, well, as I was saying, as Sinbad crossed the desert sands beside some variety of tree or other and passed some large stone ediface or other, he reached the banks of the Nile—

"Aha!" he interrupts again, "I know your game, I'm wise to you—the Nile flowing smoothly along, but I bounce awkwardly up and down, right? Well, I can't help the way I walk, and I spit on your smooth running rivers!"

Well, I'm going to wipe off the spit, Sinbad, and not say anything about your aim—and not say any more about the story of the camel, either.

"Dromedary!" screams Sinbad, "And it would have been a lousy story anyway!" and bursts into tears.

THE PROPHET AND THE MOUNTAIN

There was a mountain, once, that heard a prophet call and went immediately to the desert to answer him. "Yes, prophet?" said the mountain grandly, rising high from the desert floor directly in front of the kneeling prophet.

"Hmmm?" said the prophet distractedly, interrupted in his reveries, "Oh, yes, mountain...uh, now, what was it exactly I wanted from you?" He grimaced in painful thought while the mountain waited patiently.

"Perhaps," suggested the mountain helpfully, "You wanted to sit atop my shoulders to be closer to God's ear with your prayers?"

"Uh?" said the prophet, "Oh, I see, yes—good idea; but no, that wasn't what I wanted—God's ear is close to the ground."

"Well," said the mountain, "Perhaps, in a poetic mood, you wished to provide a seat for God, that He could converse with you in comfort?"

"Nice idea, very pretty," said the prophet, "But God is the seat of reality and needs no other."

The mountain was silent for a moment. Then it giggled: "Perhaps then, since God speaks through his seat of reality to you, my journey here was His

54

vowel movement?"

"Heh-heh," chuckled the prophet, "Pretty good, pretty. . . ."—and just then a lightning bolt struck him on his own seat, and he leaped in pain upon the side of the mountain which carried him in great haste back to its place in things, and the holy desert was silent.

Except for a long exasperated sound, which may have only been the wind.

THE BOULDER ON THE BEACH

All morning long the waves swirled curiously around the one big grey boulder all alone on the beach. Finally they summoned up the courage to ask, "Excuse, please, sir, but what do you feel that we don't?"

The elephant-sized boulder thought a moment, then replied, "Is that a riddle? I'm not very good at riddles."

"No, no," the waves all chorused, giggling, "We thought there must be something wonderful here that you feel and we don't, else why would you stay here so long?"

The boulder considered this for a while, then replied, "It *is* a riddle, isn't it? Let me guess—is the answer 'the waves'—what I feel that you don't is *you*?"

The waves all giggled again and splashed about, then asked, "Do we feel so wonderful to you, then?"

"Well," said the boulder carefully, "You sometimes tickle a bit—and in a great storm you shake me almost vigorously—but mostly my feelings are a little numbed by the rhythm of nudges and slaps that you deal me."

The waves whirled about in consideration of this, and withdrew to whisper in secret together, then

56

returned with a splash to ask, "Then why do you stay here so long, as this place is so ordinary and almost a bore?"

The boulder seemed jarred from some sleep by the question as well as the splashing, and pondered a while before replying, "Again I'm afraid I don't understand—is there a pun on 'bore'—am I shaped like a pig?"

"No, no!" leaped the waves in frustration, "We just want to know why you *stay* here."

"Oh," said the boulder, "Oh, I see—well, it's simply because I *am* here; I am the here of this place." The waves had no reply to this; they came in and washed against the big boulder, then went out to sea a little way, then came in again, and went out again, over and over, for a long time.

Soon the day grew late, the tide began to turn, and the waves began to depart into the sea, to go somewhere else.

"Come with us, boulder!" they whispered urgently, "Come with us out to sea!"

The boulder seemed to wake up again, and replied to the waves, "How nice you are to ask!—but I am *here*, you understand, and so must decline your invitation," as he watched the waves play further and farther away.

"Come away with us," they kept calling, "Come with us out to sea!" But the boulder merely smiled at

57

them in a friendly way, and then they were gone out to sea, and it was dark.

Soon the moon arose, a thin silver eyelid squinting over the horizon into the dark night. "Are you here, boulder?" asked the moon.

"I am here, moon, said the boulder, "Always here."

And the thin gaze of the moonlight found the boulder: "Ah," said the moon, "So you are," and began to slide slowly across the night sky.

The stars laughed and played in their well-mannered fashion behind the moon's back, and called to the moon, "Too fast! Too fast!" when they fell behind.

"Just watch the boulder," called the moon, "And you won't get lost but older."

"Where's the boulder?" called the stars, "Where's the boulder?"

"I'm here," said the boulder, "Always here."

But the stars blinked and blinked close to tears and called, "Too far, too far—can't see, can't see!"

"Then watch me," called the moon, "And I'll watch the boulder." And the stars and the moon swung slowly around the big boulder as the night wore away. "Goodnight, boulder," called the moon and it dipped into the sea, "Goodnight, goodnight!" chorused the stars.

"Goodbye, good trip," said the boulder sleepily, as the sky began to pale and then grow light.

58

"Morning, boulder," said the sun briskly as it peeked over the world, "Are you there?"

"I'm here, sun," said the boulder, "Always here."

"Yes yes," said the sun. "I can see you quite clearly," and immediately rose into the sky.

The tide turned again, and the waves returned: "Hi, boulder, hi, hi!" they all chorused "Still here? Still here?"

"Still here," replied the boulder smiling, "Always here."

"Oh, you should have come with us, old boulder," they splashed against him happily, "We had such a fine time, fine time!"

"That's good," replied the boulder, "Very nice," and soon seemed asleep in the midst of the play of the waves, but continued to here everything there, even so.

A SAILOR ON THE CUP

There is a white cup in our cupboard (at least it's white when it's clean; when not, it will be found on the dining room table or in the sink) that has a sailor on its side, leaning slightly forward and looking off intently to the left with his right hand shielding his eyes to look the further, his light blue bell-bottom trousers and red-and-white neckerchief flapping a bit in some invisible white breeze. How earnestly he gazes off around the cup!

Turn the cup around slowly to see what he is spying at—and you come to his own back! But why does the sailor stare around the white cup at his own back? The only possible—at least, most likely—answer is, he doesn't recognize himself from the rear! (Would you?) Ah, sailor, steadfast in your looking, how lonely you would be, on the round white cup of a world, if you knew you were only looking at yourself looking at yourself!

It is good, then, we must admit, that the sailor is not familiar with his back, and that he must assume it is *another* sailor—perhaps one he knows, perhaps a shipmate. "Ahoy!" the sailor calls to himself, and hearing the call around the cup, the sailor turns around to see who can be calling him—not recog-

60

nizing his own shout, of course. And when he turns around, what does he see? Why, another sailor turned around to answer the "ahoy" of course—himself!

"Ahoy, mate!" he calls again, and again hears his own voice at his back, and again turns to answer it—to see another sailor's back! "What nonsense is *this*?" the sailor must have asked himself (we must surmise—we did not hear him), "To call and be called and yet see nothing but backs!" Absurd, yes, but of course the sailor doesn't know he is *alone* on the cup; thinks in fact he's in a crowd of sailors playing practical jokes on him, jokes that will last until he can turn around fast enough to see their faces, at which time they will all laugh delightedly together (himself included, for sailors love a prank!), and go somewhere to have a beer—what a nice thing for a sailor to anticipate!

And so for weeks now, none of us could ever be sure which way the sailor would be looking when we would use the white cup—and indeed we are no longer sure which way he was facing in the first place! And though it is pleasant to contemplate how he thinks he is playing a bit with his mates before joining them in a laugh (how sailors can laugh!) and a glass of beer, still, it is a bit sad, somehow, knowing (as the sailor did not) that he was alone on the cup. And we had long discussions about which was better, to embrace the illusion of happy company or to recognize the truth of one's terrible aloneness . . .

61

Which became more than a little depressing, until someone's twin pointed out that you couldn't be sure that the sailor you first see, when turning the cup around, is the same sailor as the next sailor you see, since you can't see both sailors at once; nor, continuing to turn the cup, can you be sure the third sailor is the same one as the first or second you saw—and so on. And he, the someone's twin, was himself convinced that they were all *different* sailors—a whole crowd of them!

We all quickly agreed, and went somewhere for a glass of beer.

THE MAN WHO FISHED FOR COMPLIMENTS

There was once an unattached young man who fished for compliments. He bought all the most tasteful equipment, rods, reels, lures, tailored fishing costumes, and all, and earnestly studied all the most tasteful techniques. Then, all prepared, he would go every day to the pond, stand in a prominent place, and cast his line with a grace and style that caused people to say, "Oh, my, but you're a splendid fisherman!" Then he would go home, simmer the compliment in a little butter, squeeze a few drops of lemon juice on it, and eat it for dinner.

What a pleasant life! And yet, after a time, the young man found he was a bit restive, and even a bit unhappy. It all seemed so mechanical, somehow, to do his bit and be paid his compliment and go to dinner—he felt his life was lacking in some whatever it takes to make a man feel complete and realized. And his work soon reflected his unhappiness—he had to fish longer and longer each day before he was paid a compliment and could go home to fix it, say, rolled in cornmeal and fried lightly in bacon grease with a little parsley on the side.

And, probably because he had to fish so long for

64

his compliment each day, one day late in the day his tired arm let the fishline fall into the pond and stay there too long, and he caught a goldfish. The young man was dumbfounded. He stared at the goldfish incredulously for he had never seen a real fish before. As a matter of fact, he stared at it so long the goldfish had to make little noises in its throat to call his attention to its plight. "Oh, I *beg* your pardon," said the young man, and quickly took the goldfish off the hook, then tenderly put a small band-aid on its cut mouth, and helped it into a paper cup of fresh water. The goldfish's mouth was too sore for it to smile, but it nodded its head in thanks, then closed its eyes to rest from the ordeal.

    The young man felt awkward and confused. With a paper cup of sleeping goldfish in one hand and his fishing pole in the other, he stood beside the pond and pondered: he couldn't very well return the goldfish to the water, because with its injured mouth—which he was responsible for—it might not be able to eat, and could even die of starvation before the wound healed.

    "So," he said aloud to no one in particular, although a crowd had gathered and was watching him expectantly, "I will have to take this goldfish home with me and take care of it, at least until it's well again and able to return to the pond, if it so wishes." And he was then startled to hear applause from the crowd, and compliments such as "Good

65

man!" and "Well done," and "What a nice young man!"

But the young man frowned and left without a word, with something like annoyance, for he was now so happily consumed by real concerns (the goldfish here tried a little groan and was pleased by the results) that he no longer had any stomach for compliments.

THE MAN WHO LOST HIS DREAM

One evening a man we all know happened to glance across the room at the desk where his dream was to write a novel, and saw that the chair was empty. Puzzled, he recalled that often his dream was to stand on the front porch to scan the skies and consider eternity, but he found the front porch empty. He went into the den which was filled with brand new books his dream was to read, but the den was empty, too.

Alarmed, he hastened to the hallway where his dream was to exercise nightly to be fit and trim—nothing—and, quickly, across the house to the kitchen where a remodeling job was long planned—nothing again. Not up the dark street taking a late, brisk walk, not concentrating beside the radio listening to a late night symphony, not in a brightly-lit corner with sketch book in hand—nowhere.

Frightened, exhausted, and terribly alone, the man finally went into the bedroom and pulled the covers back on his bed—and there was his dream, fast asleep!

With a sigh of relief, he laid himself gently down beside it, and put his arms tenderly around it and held it close. Finally, by whispering "tomorrow" and "someday" over and over, he was able to wake it up.

THE MAN WHO MADE HIMSELF A HOUSE

There was once a man who thought to make himself a house. He was tired of travelling always and never arriving anywhere at all, and lately he had been having a terrible feeling of emptiness, as though he was disappearing from the inside out. He stopped in the empty place where he always seemed to be, stepped off the road that led from there to there, and said to himself, "Here."

Leaving room for a door at his heart and two eave windows in the roof for his eyes, he made a house of himself and built a stairway and porch and painted it all white with rather black trim. He roofed himself in slate, put glass in the windows, hung a door and then locked it, and put shades on the windows which he pulled down. "Now," he said, and waited very quietly to begin to feel at home.

After what seemed to be a terribly long time, because nothing happened and nobody visited nor even passed by, the man considered: his house was secure enough, but it was too empty to be more than simply here. And so he put up a sign in front of his house, "Vacancy—room for rent" which upon reconsideration he changed to "for lease", then to "for sale", and finally simply "Room available".

70

It wasn't any time at all before a young widow with two small children paused in front of his house to read his sign. When the man saw this, he quickly added "no children", and the widow quietly went away. Then an old man with an old dog stopped, and beside him an old woman with a cat—and the sign was quickly amended to read "or pets". Next a merry young couple, laughing and talking together, paused in front of the sign, to which was added "or noise" right before their eyes.

Soon the sign was so large with additions it all but hid the house, for "or Indians" was followed by "or Cowboys", and "or Cops" by "or Robbers", "or Peddlers" by "or Agents", and so on until everyone was excluded except the man himself.

A long silence followed, and another, and the man considered: this was worse than merely being somewhere, for here he was hidden behind his sign and couldn't see out—he started feeling the inside-out emptiness again, and became very frightened. So he quickly tore down the sign, and before a breeze could dissipate him like a pile of dead leaves, a widow with two childen and an old man with a dog and an old woman with a cat and a merry young couple opened the door at his heart and came in, and an Indian and a cowboy and a cop and a robber and a peddler and an agent and many more followed until not even a tornado would have troubled his house. And they all made themselves at home.

71

During the years that followed, day crowding upon day, the man who made himself a house had his door nearly unhinged with a thousand openings and closings, his rooms so crowded and noisy that his very foundations groaned, a window or two broken, a number of leaks in his now sagging roof— in fact, the house was falling apart! But late at night, when it was finally quiet and he could ache in peace, it didn't bother him much at all, because he was content finally to disappear like this, from the outside in, with his heart the last to go.

THE MAN AND HIS LEFT HAND

There was once a man whose left hand came to dislike him. "How have I offended you?" the man would ask his hand after it would irritably drop a cup of coffee on the floor (leaving an unsightly stain and splashing against the white walls). The hand would grow rigid as if to say, "Don't blame *me* for your carelessness!", and refuse any offers of reconciliation. And when the man each morning was all dressed up and pretty, prepared to meet the world, he would notice the left hand dangling down with no apparent interest at all in his appearance. "Would you like to wear a small ruby ring?" the man would invite politely. The hand would not deign to reply, and when the man would place the ring handsomely on its fourth finger, ah, the hand would hang even more indifferently than before, now calling attention to its detachment by the red ruby ring— like a stop light on a lonely corner where there are no cars.

It wasn't that the hand was disobedient—it did what the man instructed it to do, albeit awkwardly— but to use the left hand the man had to *monitor* it. And when he didn't use it, it just hung down from his shoulder like a sausage.

74

"I just don't understand it," mused the man, "Because the *right* hand—which is exactly the same age as the left—is *most* enthusiastic and competent!" For the man's right hand was a continuing source of great comfort to him, showing initiative and constantly doing helpful things unasked—stroking his chin, drumming musically on the table, scratching his head even when it didn't itch, pulling up his socks, snapping its fingers in simple cheerfulness, and so on. "And why does a person need two hands, anyway?" the man asked himself. "Surely one hand, of the right's calibre, would be sufficient!"

And so the man began to use only his right hand, leaving the left entirely alone and left out, perhaps to reconsider its unfriendliness—if only out of sheer boredom! But, alas, how the man was conscious of the *weight* of the unfriendly left hand. When he put it casually away in his pocket, as he had seen done by famous movie stars, the hand would go so limp that the man's whole suit would soon be pulled awry! Desperate, the man finally scolded his left hand hotly (and who can say that correction and abuse was not precisely what the wayward hand deserved?): "Now see here!" said the man, "You know, hand, your behavior is *most* discourteous and, by all standards of conduct, uncalled for! If there is some grievance you have against me, I demand you keep it a secret no longer, that it may be amended! I have no wish to see you so unhappy, and

75

I would have us amiable colleagues again: what *is* the cause of your animosity and morose behavior?" But the hand absolutely ignored him.

The man was flabbergasted, for he had expected (hoped?) the hand would be abashed by such a direct rebuke and hesitantly admit it felt neglected by the man's favoritism of his *right* hand, wanting its share of shaking hands with interesting people, writing witty notes with the fountain pen, opening doors, and so on—the man had certainly not expected such glacial contempt! And he became indignant. "Such impertinence!" he said to himself over and over, "Such *cheek*!"

Consequently, the man gave up on the left hand altogether. He wrapped it neatly in a white bandage and put it in a sling which he placed smartly around his neck. "No," he said to all his friends, "I don't think it's *broken*, exactly—just twisted or something—don't give it a thought." And his friends were delightfully sympathetic: "Bad luck!" they all said, "But at least, old man, it's not your *right* hand!" And the man would murmur, "Yes, yes, it could have been worse."

But after only a few weeks of this, he had to think of something else, for everyone would expect the hand to *heal*, sooner or later. So, inspired, the man took to carrying a briefcase everywhere he went, which he attached to his idle left hand with a small chain and padlock. "Courier duty," he

76

whispered confidentially to everyone, "Hush-hush." "Oh!" everyone whispered back, impressed, "Yes— mum's the word!" and thought him quite important.

    Everything went swimmingly for the man then, and he began to congratulate himself on his ability to rise above the sort of petty betrayals that beleaguer and defeat so many others—but then he became gradually aware that not one but both *feet* looked strange, somehow. They seemed not to fit into his shoes quite correctly, as if, perhaps, they disapproved of his *taste* in shoes! He bought new shoes— a number of them—but the problem seemed to worsen. "It's odd," the man murmured to himself, "But I never noticed how far *away* my feet are—from my head, I mean. And how mechanically they seem to behave!" It was all so baffling! He began to massage his feet each morning in the gentlest fashion, and wore none but the softest leather—yet it was not long before he was tripping over small objects and stumbling off curbs. In fact, his legs themselves seemed all wrong, somehow—like puppet legs!

    And then his belly, and elbows—soon every part of his body including his face (oh, especially the face!) seemed foreign and not to be *his* at all; in fact, he began to think he had somehow become imprisoned in the wrong body!

    But how could such a thing be? It was the same body he had always had, he knew—it was just that it

77

had grown *away* from him somehow—he no longer felt he knew it, they no longer seemed to share the same life! Oh, and it was so sad, too—it had been such a *grand* body, before, and such a good friend to him! Now, at best, it was a reluctant companion, and betrayed him in a thousand ways when he wasn't looking. It got so that he had to shout at it to get it out of bed in the mornings, and it refused to eat practically anything but oatmeal mush or a little warm broth or bread soaked in milk! And just when the man was at the end of his patience with such a body, and had just about decided to give up on it altogether, it up and died on him!

"Oh, body!" said the man then, "Is *this* what it's all about!"

"I'm so very sorry," the body replied at long last, "I tried as hard as I could, but..."

"There, there, old friend," said the man, "I should have realized—I was *blind*, that's all, and—"

"No matter, no matter," said the body, "All's well now, my friend."

"Oh, yes," said the man, "Yes! I'm just so glad to have found you again!" And he hugged his body to him with a deep sigh of gratitude, and accompanied it quite happily into the grave.

THE DISCOVERER OF FLIGHT

There was once a stout old man who stopped suddenly in the midst of his big new car and vice-presidency of something and family and all, and announced as if interrupted by some enlightenment, "I'm going to stop eating until I weigh seventeen pounds and then fly away." "Ha,ha,ha," everybody laughed; "Ha,ha,ha."

A few quiet weeks later he was noticeably thinner. "How much do you weigh now?" people would ask. "One hundred and thirty-five," he would answer; "I'm not going to eat at all any more until I reach seventeen pounds, and then fly away." "Ha,ha,ha," people would laugh, "Ha,ha,ha," and drive their big cars away.

It wasn't long before he was quite skinny. Old friends from the place he'd been vice-president of would come to see him and ask, "How much do you weigh now?" "Ninety-three," he would answer; "Soon I'll weigh seventeen pounds, and then I'll fly away." "Ha,ha,ha," they would laugh, telling this to their stout large families at the dinner table, "Ha,ha,ha."

When he weighed fifty-two pounds, prosperous doctors and specialists in nutrition would ask him for clues to his puzzling loss of appetite. "I want to

80

weigh seventeen pounds so I can fly away," he would tell them. "Ha,ha,ha," they would laugh after comparing complex theories of appetite with each other and remembering his answer, "Ha,ha,ha," they laughed.

The day finally came, fast and faster, when he weighed only eighteen—no, seventeen and three-quarters pounds, and losing rapidly. All the prosperous doctors and friends and family were crowded in his bedroom—his was a puzzling, fascinating departure, and he was as well leaving a large estate behind him. The prosperous high churchman muttered a few respectable prayers, then paused, and with a smile leaned over the old man's bed and whispered loudly enough for all to hear, "Why has this happened to you?"

The old man, too weak to speak, faintly smiled and fluttered his eyelashes like two butterflies. "Ha,ha,ha," everybody laughed until the tears of their laughter blinded them, "Ha,ha,ha." And when they had all wiped their eyes and said to each other, "Ha,ha, oh dear, ha," they looked at the bed, and the old man was gone, and the curtains were fluttering in the open window like a parting gesture.